CONTENTS

0687871

658 M

INTRODUCTION

ARE YOU MANAGING?

Are you managing your business ...

or is your business managing you?

Do you **plan** what you are going to do ...   or just react?

FAILURE TO PLAN

Has this happened in your business?

Why did it happen?

CO-ORDINATE AND CONTROL

Planning is essential for businesses to **co-ordinate** and **control** their activities.

Co-ordinate

Businesses are run by a group of individuals, each of whom will have a personal view of the best way ahead.

If there is no agreement on where the business is going, and how it will get there, the team cannot pull together.

Control

Businesses need to measure their progress against their plan in order to reassess how they are going to arrive at the agreed destination.

CLASSIC CLICHÉS

"I'm too busy to plan" ... perhaps you're too busy because you don't plan!

"My boss plans. I get on with it" ... but are you pulling in the same direction as the rest of the team?

"Just get the sales" ... which sales? Are they profitable? Will the business be worth winning?

"What's the point? Things never go according to plan" ... by planning you are focused on the future and will respond quicker to the changing environment.

PLANNING IS FOR EVERYONE!

Remember

Even the smallest cog in the largest wheel has a vital role to play in the planning process.

Don't underestimate the significance of your contribution ... and the damage that can be inflicted if you get it wrong!

FINANCIAL PLANNING

FINANCIAL PLANNING

WHAT IS A BUDGET?

A budget is a management tool which underpins the planning and control process within the business.

Definition:

A budget is telling your money

- Where to go

- Instead of worrying where it went

FINANCIAL PLANNING

IS IT NECESSARY?

- Is there a need to budget?

- Is it necessary to plan the finances?

YES!

A business is a sophisticated
money-making machine.

Don't leave it to chance!

FINANCIAL PLANNING

NEED TO PLAN

Businesses have financial responsibilities

- to their owners
- to lenders
- to employees   **These responsibilities must be planned!**
- to suppliers
- to customers

Businesses must plan **Profit** and **Cash**.

- Will the business be successful?
- Will it meet its responsibilities?
- Will it satisfy the expectations of the owners?
- **Will it be worth the effort?**

FINANCIAL PLANNING

LONG-TERM AND SHORT-TERM PLANNING

- Businesses must plan for the long-term (the Strategic Plan) as well as the short-term (the Business Plan)

- The **Strategic Plan** sets the 'vision' of where the business wants to be in 3-5 years' time

- The **Business Plan** sets out the steps the business needs to take **now** in order to move towards the strategic aims

- Financial Planning will be detailed at the business plan level, more of an 'overview' at the strategic level

FINANCIAL PLANNING

PLANNING FOR PROFIT
WHERE TO START

- You need to persuade people to invest

- You need to examine the markets

- You need to design products/services

- You need to select facilities -
  the tools to do the job

But you start with a plan!

PLANNING FOR PROFIT
WHERE TO START

- People will not invest
- Banks will not lend money

Unless it is clear: - why you need the money

- that the scheme is viable

- that the financial outcome will meet your expectations and theirs

You start with a business plan

FINANCIAL PLANNING

PLANNING FOR PROFIT
THE BUSINESS PLAN

The Business Plan should 'set the scene' and state the short-term objectives.

'Setting the scene'

- What will be your products/markets?
- Who will be your competitors? What will they be doing?
- Economic factors - inflation, interest rates, exchange rates, etc
- Technological changes - affecting your processes and/or markets

Short-term objectives

What are you planning to achieve in the short-term?

- Products - existing/new products
- Markets - existing/new customers
- Processes - existing/new methods of supply
- Employees - changes to skills-base

FINANCIAL PLANNING

PLANNING FOR PROFIT

THE BUSINESS FINANCIAL MODEL

The Business Financial Model explains how money works within the business.
Financial planning involves managing the model forward... not just letting it happen.

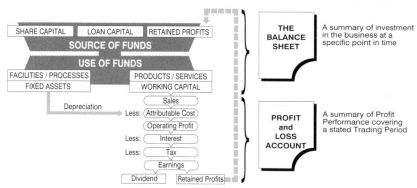

See further Appendix One.

PLANNING FOR PROFIT

LOGISTICS FLOW

Where do I enter the model?

Start with the products or services you are planning to sell. Think how you process and deliver them to your customer.

Example

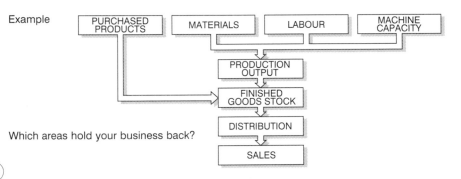

```
PURCHASED          MATERIALS      LABOUR       MACHINE
PRODUCTS                                       CAPACITY
                          │
                          ▼
                    PRODUCTION
                      OUTPUT
                          │
                          ▼
                    FINISHED
                  GOODS STOCK
                          │
                          ▼
                   DISTRIBUTION
                          │
                          ▼
                      SALES
```

Which areas hold your business back?

FINANCIAL PLANNING

PLANNING FOR PROFIT
LIMITING FACTOR

● Identify the limiting factor

This is usually sales - but could be capacity, labour skills availability, etc.

The limiting factor can change from year to year, eg:

Limiting factor	What if you:-
SALES	- spend more on advertising - cut the selling price of the product
CAPACITY	- purchase extra machinery - sub-contract work
LABOUR SKILLS	- increase wages - recruit from other labour markets (eg: overseas)

Part of the challenge process (see page 26) is to argue these 'what-ifs?'.

FINANCIAL PLANNING

PLANNING FOR PROFIT

LIMITING FACTOR

● Having identified the limiting factor you can now start to plan:

What income will I receive? - **the Sales Budget**

What will I need to spend in order to deliver the sales and achieve the other short-term objectives? - **the Expenditure Budgets**

Note: CASH CAN ALSO BE THE LIMITING FACTOR! See page 24.

PLANNING FOR PROFIT

THE SALES BUDGET

The sales budget is driven by sales forecasts ... compiled by sales people.

- Traditionally sales forecasts are optimistic!
- You need to take into account:

    - Price(s)
    - Volume(s)
    - Mix of product
    - Timing

- The budget must be phased to assess capacity/workload implications
- Don't forget to allow for customer credit in budgeting cash receipts
- Challenge each of the components planned in the light of:

    - the total market   - track record   - the competition

Note: The sales budget must be set in sufficient detail to allow the expenditure budgets to be formulated sensibly. In a one-product business this is straight-forward. In a multi-product business where products have dramatically different expenditure implications, a detailed analysis of the planned sales is essential.

FINANCIAL PLANNING

PLANNING FOR PROFIT

THE EXPENDITURE BUDGETS

Planned expenditure is classified as **Capital** or **Revenue**.

Capital Budget — planned expenditure on the processes/facilities (Fixed Assets)

Revenue Budget — planned expenditure on the materials, labour and running costs of the business

Compiling **Capital Budgets** and **Revenue Budgets** is dealt with in detail in later sections of the pocketbook.

However - do be careful!

Capital and revenue budget-setting can be mistakenly seen as separate activities - but each can have implications on the other, eg:

- buying a new machine (**Capital**) will affect maintenance, power, insurance, etc (**Revenue**)
- using outside hauliers (**Revenue**) will obviate the need for new delivery vans (**Capital**)

Be consistent!

FINANCIAL PLANNING

PLANNING FOR PROFIT

LINK TO THE MODEL

Now feed the sales budget and expenditure budgets into the model.

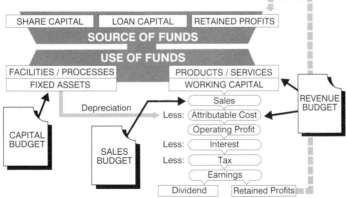

SHARE CAPITAL | LOAN CAPITAL | RETAINED PROFITS
SOURCE OF FUNDS
USE OF FUNDS
FACILITIES / PROCESSES | PRODUCTS / SERVICES
FIXED ASSETS | WORKING CAPITAL

CAPITAL BUDGET

Depreciation

SALES BUDGET

REVENUE BUDGET

Sales
Less: Attributable Cost
Operating Profit
Less: Interest
Less: Tax
Earnings
Dividend | Retained Profits

(21)

PLANNING FOR PROFIT
HAVE YOU MADE A PROFIT?

Use your product costing system to determine:

- given your revenue budget
- what will be the budgeted cost of your products?

And having set your sales budget

- will you make a profit on the products you plan to sell?

Note: Product costing systems are explained in a later section of the pocketbook.

FINANCIAL PLANNING

PLANNING FOR PROFIT

FINANCING COSTS

You are now in a position to complete the model by feeding in the budget for interest, tax and dividends.

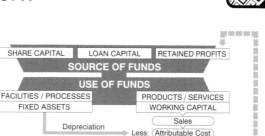

Don't forget to review the Source of Funds.

- Will you need additional share capital and/or loan capital?
- Have you remembered to adjust dividends/interest accordingly?

Repeat until the model is in equilibrium.

PLANNING FOR CASH

Businesses need cash in order to survive.

Without cash you cannot pay for materials, or labour, or services.
Without cash the profit-making machine will grind to a halt.
Profit is not the same thing as cash

- You must plan the cash as well as the profit.
- Many profitable businesses end up in liquidation!
- Therefore, just planning for profit is not good enough!

Note that the cash plan - the cashflow forecast - is an
integral part of the budget review process.
Never approve a budget plan unless the cashflow forecast
has been reviewed and is acceptable.

The business graveyard is littered with 'successful' businesses which ran out of cash.

Be warned!

The difference between profit and cash, and cashflow forecasting is explained in *The Managing Cashflow Pocketbook*.

FINANCIAL PLANNING

EVALUATE THE OUTCOME

Now assess your plan. Is it good enough? Look at the expected outcome.

Will the plan enable the business to meet its financial responsibilities to its:
- owners: dividends, share price growth
- lenders: interest, capital repayments
- employees: wages, salaries, secure employment
- suppliers: payment, continued 'partnership'
- customers: quality, availability, service, warranty

Will the result enable the business to progress towards its strategic aims?
If not ... go back to the drawing-board!

Remember this is a **plan** - if the expected outcome is unsatisfactory you have the chance
to redirect the business ... before it is too late!

FINANCIAL PLANNING

THE CHALLENGE PROCESS

You now submit (or formally present) your budget. Next comes the challenge process - ideally carried out by a team who have not been involved in the previous stages.

- Is the budget consistent?
  - have the same assumptions been used throughout?
- Are those assumptions valid?
- What are the critical success factors? What are the risks involved? ie:
  - which events/outcomes are the key determinants in achieving the budgeted result?
- Are the budgeted returns worth the risks?
- **Could you do better?**

The budget may be re-worked many times before agreement is reached.

FINANCIAL PLANNING

CONTINUOUS REVIEW

The future is uncertain.

Planning enables the business to be proactive - but you will still be unable to dictate your own destiny precisely.

Don't bury your head in the sand!

Continuously review your plans:

- what new opportunities have arisen?
- new threats?
- what are the financial implications?

Managing a business requires you to be in **control**. Being in control means you can respond to changes in circumstances.

Keep looking forward!

FINANCIAL PLANNING

INTER-RELATIONSHIPS

The following sections of the book examine some of the key elements of
financial planning:

- Revenue budgets
- Capital budgets
- Product costing

Whilst these are often viewed as separate
exercises within the business, do not
overlook the complex inter-relationships.

For example, the decision to purchase a new machine will have a ripple effect, changing
the capital budget, revenue budget, sales budget (if customers buy more or pay more)
and cash budget.

View each of the budgets as part of the whole.

REVENUE BUDGETS

REVENUE BUDGETS

AIM

The Revenue Budget sets out the expenditure plans for the running costs of the business.

- What are we trying to achieve?
  - an effective and efficient allocation of resources to achieve the company plan
- What do many businesses have?
  - a discredited process which everyone ignores!

Why?

Recognise any of the following?

REVENUE BUDGETS

THE BUDGET SABOTEURS!

1 *"Nobody asked my opinion ... even a half-wit should have realised that we'd need extra maintenance work"*

2 *"You want me to set my budget? I've got customers screaming, suppliers on strike ... say £10,000 and leave me to get on with my real job"*

3 *"My budget for next year? What have I spent this year?"*

4 *"I'll need £9,000 ... I'd better add £1,000 for contingencies, and last year they cut all budgets by 8%, so I'll top it up by 10% just in case ... Tell them £11,000"*

5 *"If my budget gets smaller I'll lose status in the organisation"*

6 *"That's finished the budget then. Let's pass it to the accountant and it's her problem for the next 12 months"*

7 *"If I don't spend everything in my budget I won't get as much next year"*

8 *"As long as I stay within budget, nobody will ask me any questions"*

GOLDEN RULES OF BUDGETING

1: Draw everyone into the process. Build a team solution to a team challenge.

DON'T make budgeting a top-level activity

DO involve everyone who is responsible for spending the business's money

- they have 'hands on' knowledge of where resources will be required
- involvement encourages them to 'buy into' the plan
- if they are to be responsible for the outcome they must have a role in determining the resources available to them

- Commitment to the ownership of the figures in the budget plays an important part in making them achievable during the year

NOBODY ASKED MY OPINION .. EVEN A HALF-WIT...

GOLDEN RULES OF BUDGETING

2: Budgets are a key part of the planning process. Invest sufficient time to do them properly!

DON'T underestimate the importance of budget setting ... it **IS** a **VITAL** part of your job

DO take sufficient time to set the budget properly

- Setting a budget properly requires you to formulate your plans; this will help with day-to-day decisions as well

- Too low a budget and you spend the next year trying to achieve the impossible

- Too high a budget and you deprive others of valuable resources they could have used to benefit the business

> I'VE GOT CUSTOMERS SCREAMING, SUPPLIERS ON STRIKE ...

GOLDEN RULES OF BUDGETING

3: Budgets allocate resources to meet future needs. Keep looking ahead!

DON'T base the future on the past

DO look at what you need to achieve in the budget period

- Making comparison with last year - applying a small across the board increase - is a common method of budgeting; it is one way of finding a starting place, **but it is not enough**

- How many businesses assume next year will be the same as this year - and survive to tell the tale!

- Planning is not easy - next year **will** be different ... in what ways?

WHAT HAVE
I SPENT
THIS YEAR?

GOLDEN RULES OF BUDGETING

4: Budgets allocate scarce resources to competing needs. Don't ask for more than you need!

DON'T pad budgets

DO budget on a 'most likely' basis

- Clearly state the budget assumptions

- Explain resource implications of alternative scenarios

- Budget padding turns the budget process into a game - the business will be the loser

BETTER ADD £1,000 FOR CONTINGENCIES, AND I'LL TOP IT UP JUST IN CASE OF CUTS ...

(35)

REVENUE BUDGETS

GOLDEN RULES OF BUDGETING

5: The successful manager is not the one with the largest budget; he or she is the one who makes best use of the budget available.

DON'T measure people by the size of their budgets!

DO judge them by how effectively and efficiently they use the resources available to them

- Condemn empire-building
- Change parochial attitudes aimed at 'protecting' the department
- Promote the team approach

GOLDEN RULES OF BUDGETING

6: Time is a continuum. Budgeting, planning for the future, must also be a continuous process.

DON'T make budgeting an annual activity

DO have a process of continual review and revision

- Re-examine and revise budgets regularly to adapt to the changing business environment; eg: every quarter re-forecast and budget next twelve months

- Remember that the future is uncertain

Look what happened to the dodo!

> THAT'S FINISHED THE BUDGET — NOW IT'S THE ACCOUNTANT'S PROBLEM

(37)

GOLDEN RULES OF BUDGETING

7: Budgets are determined according to future needs - not this year's spend. Challenge any flurry of expenditure near year-end!

DON'T waste valuable resources in a misguided attempt to protect your budget for the next year

DO inform others so that the extra resources can be usefully deployed elsewhere

- Remember - next year's budget should be based on next year's need **NOT** this year's spend!

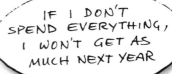

IF I DON'T SPEND EVERYTHING, I WON'T GET AS MUCH NEXT YEAR

REVENUE BUDGETS

GOLDEN RULES OF BUDGETING

8: **Budgets allocate resources based on current priorities and anticipated costs. These priorities and costs may change.**

DON'T see the budget as a 'licence to spend'

DO review all expenditure
- is it still necessary?
- is this the best way?
- have priorities changed?

- Challenge all expenditure!

- Releasing resources can resolve problems elsewhere in the business

AS LONG AS I STAY WITHIN BUDGET, NOBODY WILL ASK ANY QUESTIONS

GOLDEN RULES OF BUDGETING
FORECAST

Successful budgeting cannot be achieved single-handed.

Everyone must be committed to the new approach.

The team may have cynics who need converting.

Evangelise! Spread the word!

Don't forget the **Forecast!**

F orward-thinking
O pen Management style
R eview continuously
E xacting
C ommitted
A daptable
S elf-critical
T eam Approach

REVENUE BUDGETS

SETTING BUDGETS

Adopt the **FORWARD PLANNING APPROACH**

Start with the statement:

"The reason I need a budget is that you need me to do something".

Then the 4 stages follow:

Stage 1: What do you need me to do?

Stage 2: How am I going to do it?

Stage 3: What resources will I need?

Stage 4: How much will these resources cost?

The Input-Output approach can guide you through these four stages.

SETTING BUDGETS

INPUT-OUTPUT ANALYSIS (I/O)

- I/O is a technique often used in TQM (Total Quality Management) where the relationship between departments is charted on a customer-supplier basis
- The technique is also useful to depict the wrong and right way to budget:

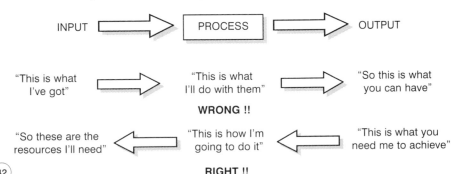

INPUT ⟹ PROCESS ⟹ OUTPUT

"This is what I've got" ⟹ "This is what I'll do with them" ⟹ "So this is what you can have"

WRONG !!

"So these are the resources I'll need" ⟸ "This is how I'm going to do it" ⟸ "This is what you need me to achieve"

RIGHT !!

REVENUE BUDGETS

SETTING BUDGETS
INPUT-OUTPUT APPROACH

INPUT ➡ PROCESS ➡ OUTPUT

Stage 1: What do you need me to do?

- Identify the **OUTPUTS**
- Clarify **what** has to be achieved and **when**, eg: make 1,000 units of product each month
    - **or** sell 500 crates every quarter
    - **or** devise an advertising campaign by December
    - **or** reduce complaints of bad quality by 20% within 12 months
    - **or** visit every customer 4 times a year

REVENUE BUDGETS

SETTING BUDGETS

INPUT-OUTPUT APPROACH

Stage 2: How am I going to do it?

- Choose the **PROCESS**, ie: the way you will achieve your **OUTPUT**
- Challenge the existing process
- Brainstorm alternatives: - use our own employees?
                            - use outside agencies?
                            - automate?
- Encourage innovative ideas from your staff

Then evaluate the alternatives and make your choice.

Stage 3: What resources will I need?

Identify the **INPUTS** you require:

People - how many?
        - which skills?
        - what hours?

Expenses - what do you need to buy? Quality? Quantity?

REVENUE BUDGETS

SETTING BUDGETS

INPUT-OUTPUT APPROACH

Stage 4: How much will these resources cost?

Only **now** do you attempt to quantify in financial terms.

This is the easy bit! Your accountant will be able to help.

People: Salary applicable to skills required
Overtime and shift premiums
Anticipated salary increases
Employment costs (National Insurance and pension contributions)

Expenses: Current prices - or obtain quotation
Predicted/known price increases

This is your budget submission!

SETTING BUDGETS

BUDGET CO-ORDINATION

The input-output approach also provides an effective tool to co-ordinate the budgets.

Remember every output should be someone's input.

'WALK' YOUR PLANNED OUTPUTS TO YOUR CUSTOMER
- is the output required?
- will it be in the format / frequency required?

Are the budgets consistently prepared?

REVENUE BUDGETS

SETTING BUDGETS
BUDGET REVISIONS

- By going through the 4 stage procedure, agreement is reached on:

  1 The outputs to be achieved   2 The process to be used

  3 The resources required for this   4 The cost of those resources
      process to achieve those outputs

- Subsequent changes to the budget must therefore correspond to:

      a change to the outputs required
  - **or** an alternative process
  - **or** a change to the resources required
  - **or** a change to the cost of those resources

- Budget credibility can be maintained with an amended balance of `Input'
  and `Output'

SETTING BUDGETS

BUDGET REVISIONS

- This structured approach should prevent the demoralising effect of indiscriminate across-the-board budget cuts

- No wonder the budgets lose credibility when such cuts are announced!

- A well-prepared budget submission is destroyed; why bother doing it properly next time?

- Some costs cannot be rationally treated this way, eg:

  a computer maintenance contract has been signed costing £5,000 a year for the next 3 years; how can you impose a 10% reduction here?

REVENUE BUDGETS

MONITORING AND CONTROLLING BUDGETS

The budget has now been agreed. Is that it? **NO**

It must now be **controlled.**

Budgetary control is often viewed as a simple closed loop system:

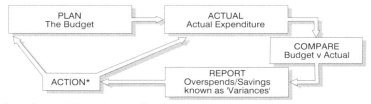

* **Action** - the most important part!

You must either:
   i) bring actual expenditure back in line with budget, or
   ii) notify a need to change the budget as a result of a permanent or on-going overspend or saving

REVENUE BUDGETS

MONITORING AND CONTROLLING BUDGETS

REPORTING THE VARIANCES

Remember the three Rs:

- Feedback from the system must be:

    - **R**apid
    - **R**egular
    - **R**eliable

- You need to identify variances quickly in order to:

    - investigate and understand why they have happened
    - understand the relationships between budgets and hence variances
      (eg: extra sales will result in additional work in the packing department and
      increased shipping costs)
    - respond effectively, either changing your actions to bring expenditure back in line
      with the budget or communicating the need to change the budget

- Don't hide your problems!

MONITORING AND CONTROLLING BUDGETS

UNDERSTANDING THE VARIANCES

- This system is not just about measuring whether you will need more money than originally planned

- Remember that the reason for allocating resources is to take actions to achieve the company objectives

    - is any saving or overspend attributable to a change in the level of performance?
    - have the plans been achieved? ... surpassed?

    The budget should never stand still! It is an allocation of resources to carry out the required actions perceived at a particular point in time

    - have the required actions changed?
    - have the business objectives changed?
    - has the strategic plan changed?

MONITORING AND CONTROLLING BUDGETS

TEAM APPROACH

Successful budgeting involves a flow of resources to and from managers as the needs of the business change.

Just because you have the money in your original budget doesn't mean you ought to spend it! Someone else may now have a more urgent need!

Encourage the team approach to optimise resource allocation.

Communication is the key!

- What new opportunities have arisen in the business?
- What new threats have appeared?
- What resources can managers offer to meet these?

REVENUE BUDGETS

MONITORING AND CONTROLLING BUDGETS

TEAM APPROACH

Departments **must not** act in isolation.

- Problems in one area can be
  - caused by actions taken in other areas
  - have implications for other budget holders

  (Remember the Input-Output analysis and the internal supplier-customer relationship.)
  See page 42

- An overspend on money-back guarantees to customers, for example, could
  - be caused by purchasing cheaper materials (does the budget saving in one area compensate the overspend elsewhere?)
  - have implications for the success of the launch of your new products

Look at such issues from an overall company perspective **NOT** from a parochial departmental view.

This can be improved by meetings where overspends are communicated and tackled as a company problem - what about monthly working lunches as a forum for such discussions?

REVENUE BUDGETS

MONITORING AND CONTROLLING BUDGETS
KEEP LOOKING FORWARD!

Accounting periods - month end, year end, etc, have an impact which is largely artificial. Businesses should not be run in this stop-start manner!

Think beyond year end!

- Rolling budgets encourage managers to continue to look ahead, enhancing the quality of the planning and helping to avoid short-term solutions

- To prepare a rolling budget, add an additional month to the budget at every month-end, thereby always looking 12 months ahead; this will also save you a lot of time and effort at the formal budget-setting period!

CAPITAL BUDGETS

CAPITAL BUDGETS

INTRODUCTION

The Revenue budget does not include Capital Expenditure.

Capital expenditure is the purchase of plant, equipment, buildings, etc (known as 'Fixed Assets') which will be used by the business over a number of years.

Capital expenditure is budgeted separately in the **Capital Budget.**

CAPITAL BUDGETS

STRATEGIC FIT

- Capital expenditure is a **strategic** investment

    - it determines the way the business will make its
      products or deliver its services for many years into
      the future

- The wrong choices will result in **competitive disadvantage**

- Reversing the decision is: **time-consuming
                              expensive**

- Hence the budgeting and approval system should be searching

- Many companies require capital expenditure to be authorised by the board

CAPITAL BUDGETS

COMPILING THE BUDGET

- The capital budget will be compiled after considering:

  Capacity   - Does the business plan necessitate additional production/distribution capacity?

  Replacement   - Which facilities need replacing; with what?

  Safety   - Is there investment required to comply with health and safety legislation?

  Efficiency   - How could overall costs be reduced?

  All this must be done in the context of the **manufacturing strategy**

  - The capital budget will be submitted to the board for approval
  - Acceptance will depend on:
    - cash availability
    - competing priorities within the company or group

CAPITAL BUDGETS

AUTHORISATION OF EXPENDITURE

- The capital budget agrees a planned level of investment

- However: **just because it is in the budget doesn't mean you can have it!**

- When the manager wishes to proceed with the investment he/she will have to submit a further evaluation

- This document is commonly called a 'Capital Appraisal Form', 'Indent', or 'CER' (Capital Expenditure Request)

- The level of detail required will vary but will usually include:

  - Details of the item to be purchased
  - Reason for recommending purchase ('the strategic logic')
  - Financial evaluation

CAPITAL BUDGETS

EVALUATING CAPITAL EXPENDITURE
THE STRUCTURED APPROACH

Each request for capital expenditure will be examined on its merits in respect of:

Strategic fit: Is the proposed expenditure consistent with the business strategy?

Risk profile: What is the resultant business risk profile - is it acceptable?

Database: How has the data been compiled? What assumptions have been used?

Financial profile: What is the anticipated financial return? Is the return worth the risk?

Management implications: Are the management resources/skills available to ensure the satisfactory completion of the project?

CAPITAL BUDGETS

LINK TO OTHER BUDGETS

LINK TO REVENUE BUDGET

Remember the inter-relationships between Capital and Revenue expenditure.

Capital expenditure	Revenue expenditure
Buildings	Rates, electricity, maintenance, depreciation *
Machinery	Power, labour, maintenance, depreciation *
Vehicles	Tax, insurance, fuel, depreciation *

The capital and revenue budgets must therefore be prepared on a consistent basis.

LINK TO SALES BUDGET

What benefit does the investment offer your customers?
Will the additional sales offset the additional revenue costs?

If they do not, your business will end up footing the bill - through reduced profits!

* Depreciation and capital and revenue expenditure are explained more fully in
 The Balance Sheet Pocketbook.

CAPITAL BUDGETS

LINK TO CASH BUDGET

Capital expenditure requires **Cash!**

It is essential to consider:

- How much will be required?
- When will it be required?
- Will sufficient funds be available?

Note: Possible finance charges should be linked to the revenue budget.

PRODUCT COSTING

PRODUCT COSTING

LINK TO BUDGETS

To win sales, the business must agree a selling price!

In most instances the customer demands to know the price before placing an order.

Therefore, a business must plan ahead to assess the expected revenue expenditure which will be incurred.

Budgets provide the management tool and the basis for assessing future costs.

PRODUCT COSTING

DO COSTS MATTER?

"As long as we are making a profit, does it matter where it comes from?"

YES!!

How much profit will you make this year?

- Will it be enough? (see page 25)
- How much profit does each of the products make?
- What are the implications of a change in sales mix?
- What will be the impact of cost increases?

Are you in control of your business?

If you want to manage profit you must
understand and control the costs of
making and selling your products.

THE PRODUCT COST

PRODUCT COSTING

WHY PRODUCT COSTS?

Product costs are used for:

- Valuing stocks
- Calculating profit
- Business decisions:
    - pricing
    - cost reduction
    - make/buy
    - capital expenditure
      evaluation
- Transfer pricing

Understanding the product cost is essential

PRODUCT COSTING

LINK TO PRICING

- In many instances **price** is not determined by **cost** but by how much the market will pay

- Where there is no established market valuation, you will use cost as the basis for

  - price lists
  - bids/tenders/quotations

If you don't understand your costs you may be turning down profitable business ... or taking on orders that will kill the business off!

Where do you get this cost information from?

The Costing System

PRODUCT COSTING

BASIS OF MANAGEMENT DECISIONS

Which are your most profitable

- Products?
- Product groups?
- Markets?
- Customers?

Your response will drive key strategic decisions:

- Which products shall we expand/drop?
- Should we increase market penetration in America?
- Can we afford to offer a discount to secure more business?
  etc

Where do you get your information for such decisions?

The Costing System

PRODUCT COSTING

COST CONTROL

- Which costs are increasing/decreasing?

- Would it be cheaper to make or sell our products in a different way?

    - using different machines
    - sub-contracting
    - using distributors, etc

- How can we design for cost?

Where do you turn to for this information?

The Costing System

PRODUCT COSTING

THE PROBLEM ... THE SOLUTION

"Can't I leave all that to the accountant?"   **No!**

WORRYING FACT: There is no such thing as **the** product cost!

Why not? Because all costing systems entail assumptions/judgements being made.

Give twelve accountants the task of costing a product and they will come up with twelve different, correct answers!

What can you do?

1   Understand the way your existing costing system works

2   Identify its strengths and weaknesses and contribute to constructive criticism aimed at overcoming the problems

3   Accept that there is no one product cost and be prepared to adjust the cost database accordingly

PRODUCT COSTING

STEP 1: UNDERSTAND THE SYSTEM

What is a costing system?

Businesses use resources to make products.

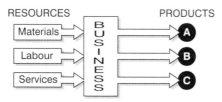

Assessing the resources is easy.
You pay for them via invoices and the payroll.

But which of the resources are used for each of the products?
The link attributing resources to products is

The Costing System

PRODUCT COSTING

UNDERSTAND THE SYSTEM
THE CONFLICT

How do accountants tackle this?
There are two types of accounting:

FINANCIAL   versus   MANAGEMENT

PRODUCT COSTING

UNDERSTAND THE SYSTEM

FINANCIAL ACCOUNTING

Primary objective: **Published accounts**

Costs required for: **Profit and loss account** (cost of sales)
Balance sheet (stock valuation)

Focus: **Backwards - reporting events that have already happened**

Criteria for Adequacy? **Compliance with accounting standards.**

Note:

- Financial accountants have rules (Statements of Standard Accounting Practice - SSAPs or Financial Reporting Standards - FRS) which they must comply with when producing published accounts
- SSAP 9 governs the method of valuing stock and hence product costing
- Published accounts are for external users and the standards aim to improve consistency in approach

But will this be appropriate for decision-making?

PRODUCT COSTING

UNDERSTAND THE SYSTEM
MANAGEMENT ACCOUNTING

Primary objective:	**To assist decision making**
Costs required for:	**Day to day operational decisions** **Medium- and long-term strategic decisions**
Focus:	**Forward - predicting cost implications**
Criteria for adequacy?	**Local relevance!**

Where do you get this decision-making information from? Is it the financial accounting system? Look at its different focus. Will it really be adequate? **Probably not!**

PRODUCT COSTING

UNDERSTAND THE SYSTEM

ELEMENTS OF COST

	£
Direct Material	xx
Direct Labour	xx
Production Overhead	xx
Product Cost	xx

- In most businesses the product costing system will have been set up to include some or all of these elements

- What do these terms mean and how are they calculated?

Direct Material
Total material consumed in producing each unit, calculated by either

    i) booking all materials against a particular job, or
    ii) having a bill of materials for products, listing the materials that must have been used *

Direct Labour
Total cost of operatives involved in adding value to the cost unit, calculated by either

    i) booking time to specific jobs, or
    ii) having a layout listing the operations that must have been carried out *

* **Note:** When producing budgeted product costs these costs have to be estimated (see page 71)

PRODUCT COSTING

UNDERSTAND THE SYSTEM
PRODUCTION OVERHEAD

What are the production overheads?

- the running costs of the manufacturing department including wages, salaries and expenses *

How are the production overheads attributed to products? **This is the tricky bit!**

- How much electricity did we use for Product A?
- How much of the managers' costs should be charged to each product?
- How much maintenance cost should be charged to Product B? etc

Accountants use the 3 A's   **A**llocation
                                  Apportionment
                                  Absorption

* **Note:** The non-manufacturing departmental costs are often excluded from the product costing system. This can be dangerous! (see page 87)

PRODUCT COSTS

UNDERSTAND THE SYSTEM

OVERHEADS: ALLOCATION

- The Production process is divided up into areas of similar types of activity called **Cost Centres**
- These could be, eg: machining, assembly, repair
- Each type of production overhead cost is then **allocated** or **apportioned** to the cost centres to arrive at an overhead cost for each cost centre

Expense	Basis of charge	Machining £'000	Assembly £'000	Repair £'000	Total £'000
Indirect Labour					300
Depreciation					270
Maintenance					160
Indirect Materials					60
Power					50
Rent					160
TOTAL					1,000

PRODUCT COSTING

UNDERSTAND THE SYSTEM

OVERHEADS: ALLOCATION AND APPORTIONMENT

- Wherever possible overheads are **allocated** to the cost centre consuming the resources, eg: if each cost centre has different supervisors, their salaries can be **allocated** to the centre in which they work

- Certain overheads will not be capable of allocation, eg: rent, power, personnel services

- An appropriate method of sharing these between the relevant cost centres must be found, ie: **apportionment**

    Example: **power** - machine rating x machine hours
    rent - area occupied
    personnel - number of employees

Be rational. Don't waste money trying to allocate small sums accurately only to apportion large amounts!

Focus on the dominant costs!

PRODUCT COSTING

UNDERSTAND THE SYSTEM

OVERHEADS BY COST CENTRE

The tabulation analysing all overheads by cost centre can now be completed.

Expense	Basis of charge	Machining £'000	Assembly £'000	Repair £'000	Total £'000
Indirect Labour	Allocation	160	80	60	300
Depreciation	Allocation	160	30	80	270
Maintenance	Allocation	80	30	50	160
Indirect Materials	Allocation	15	20	25	60
Power	Apportionment	25	5	20	50
Rent	Apportionment	60	35	65	160
TOTAL		500	200	300	1,000

PRODUCT COSTING

UNDERSTAND THE SYSTEM

OVERHEADS: ABSORPTION

- The costs of each cost centre are then charged out to the products using an **overhead absorption rate**

- The traditional approach is to use a
  labour hour rate, or **machine hour rate**

Step 1   Establish the overhead costs allocated/apportioned to the cost centre,
eg: £500,000

Step 2   Determine the number of labour (or machine) hours to be produced by the
cost centre in the year, eg: 20,000

Step 3   Calculate the overhead hourly rate, eg:

$$\frac{£500,000}{20,000} = £25/\text{hour}$$

Step 4   Charge products with overhead according to the number of hours' work
required in the cost centre, eg:

1/2 hour ⟶ £12.50 overhead

PRODUCT COSTING

UNDERSTAND THE SYSTEM

EXAMPLE

- You are invited to tender for a contract to supply Product X

- Product X will require: Direct materials £50
  Direct labour 7 hours

- Your Production Budget shows: Total Production overheads £600,000
  Planned labour hours 15,000
  Planned direct wages per hour £5

- You calculate your overhead absorption rate: $\dfrac{£600,000}{15,000 \text{ hours}}$ = £40/hour

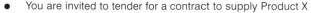

	£
Direct material	50
Direct labour (7 hours x £5)	35
Production overhead: 7 hours x £40/hour	280
Product cost	**365**

This information would play a key role in the tendering process. Is it correct? Or could there be other answers - see *Appendix Two*.

PRODUCT COSTING

STEP 2: CHALLENGE THE SYSTEM

- Look at your own costing system

- Is it deficient?

- Here are some classic indicators of problems:

    - 'easy' products are reported to be loss-makers

    - 'difficult' products are reported as highly profitable

    - competitors seem unable to match your low prices

    - competitors continually under-cut you

    - cost information is ignored/disbelieved

    - departmental PC based information is
      compiled to provide 'true costs'

PRODUCT COSTING

CHALLENGE THE SYSTEM
YOU ARE UNIQUE!

The following pages identify some of the areas to start looking at, when you challenge your own product costing system.

- The costing system should trace resources through to products (see page 71)

- No two companies use identical resources in exactly the same way to make the same products

- Hence no two costing systems should be the same!

Is your system tailored to reflect what goes on in your business?

PRODUCT COSTING

CHALLENGE THE SYSTEM
WHO WROTE IT?

- The costing system should trace resources through to products
- Who knows this process best? Probably **not** the accountant!
But who wrote the costing system?

- How often do you change the resources, processes or products?
How often does the costing system change?

- The management accountant produces cost information to facilitate decision-making
Does it really help you take better decisions?

PRODUCT COSTING

CHALLENGE THE SYSTEM
OVERHEADS

- Product costs will be affected by:

    - number and definition of cost centres
    - basis of apportioning costs
    - method of absorption

Has sufficient thought been given to the choices in your system?

A detailed example of the effect this can have on the product cost is given in Appendix Two

CHALLENGE THE SYSTEM

BELOW-THE-LINE COSTS

- Most costing systems treat direct materials, direct labour and production overhead as product-related, whereas other operating costs (expenses) are deemed to be non product-related
- These expenses are often referred to as 'below-the-line', ie: below gross profit
- This results in profit reports which only identify product profitability at the Gross Profit stage

Example

	A £	B £	Total £
Sales	100	100	200
Less:			
Cost of Goods Sold	70	50	120
Gross Profit	30	50	80
Expenses:			
Admin			10
Selling			20
Service			30
Operating Profit			20

- The business wishes to focus its product range
- Which product should it drop, A or B?
- What effect will it have on operating profit?

PRODUCT COSTING

CHALLENGE THE SYSTEM

BELOW-THE-LINE COSTS

Would your response be different if the following information were available to you?

A has been made for many years and any design/manufacturing problems eliminated. It is sold in large quantities to a few customers.

B is a new product with many teething problems. It is sold in small quantities to many different customers.

Discussions with the relevant departmental managers enable the below-the-line expenses to be analysed by product. Don't be put off! You are not looking for excessive precision in this allocation. Managers should be able to give you an approximate percentage split.

	A	B	Total
	£	£	£
Sales	100	100	200
Less:			
Cost of Goods Sold	70	50	120
Gross Profit	30	50	80
Expenses:			
Admin	2	8	10
Selling	4	16	20
Service	-	30	30
Operating Profit/(Loss)	24	(4)	20

Does your business make its strategic decisions at the gross profit stage?

PRODUCT COSTING

CHALLENGE THE SYSTEM

TIME-RELATED OVERHEADS

Traditional absorption costing implies that the overhead part of the product cost depends on time, ie: if the overhead rate is £60/hour then if Product J and K both take 10 minutes to make, they will both be charged with £10 overhead.

Is this realistic?

Are all overhead costs driven by time?

Example:
Products J and K both take 10 minutes per unit to machine. J is a long-established product; material is purchased and received in the normal batch size of 100. When J is machined, the first-off is inspected and the balance run automatically.

K is a new product. It has been badly designed and engineered. Material is purchased and received in the normal batch quantity of 1! When K is being machined, managers, designers, engineers and inspectors crowd around the machine nursing the product through the process.

PRODUCT COSTING

CHALLENGE THE SYSTEM
TIME-RELATED OVERHEADS

What goes into overhead costs?

- purchasing, receiving, inspection, etc, etc

Did J really cost the same to produce as K?

Do you have products with differing cost demands?

Activity Based Costing (ABC) seeks to remedy this problem by grouping overheads by **activity**, eg: purchasing, setting up machines, despatching and then charging products according to their demand for these activities.

PRODUCT COSTING

CHALLENGE THE SYSTEM
STANDARD COSTING

- Some businesses use standard costs, ie: pre-determined values for:

  Materials - price and quantity
  Labour - rate and hours

- Differences between the standard and actual values are reported as **variances**

- If your business uses standards:

  - Are the variances analysed by product? or
  - Are they treated as `below-the-line'? or
  - **Even worse**, are they prorated based on standard cost?

Look how it can influence your view!

PRODUCT COSTING

CHALLENGE THE SYSTEM

CHALLENGES: VARIANCES

		Products					
		ALPHA £'000	%	BETA £'000	%	TOTAL £'000	%*
Method 1 'Below-the-line' or	Sales	200		100		300	
	Standard Cost of Sales	100		50		150	
	Standard Gross Profit	100	50	50	50	150	50
	Variances					(30)	
	Actual Gross Profit					120	40
Method 2 'Prorata' or	Sales	200		100		300	
	Standard Cost of Sales	100		50		150	
	Standard Gross Profit	100		50		150	
	Variances	(20)		(10)		(30)	
	Actual Gross Profit	80	40	40	40	120	40
Method 3 'Analysed by product'	Sales	200		100		300	
	Standard Cost of Sales	100		50		150	
	Standard Gross Profit	100		50		150	
	Variances	50		(80)		(30)	
	Actual Gross Profit	150	75	(30)	(30)	120	40

* Profit figures expressed as a % of sales

Only the last analysis reveals that BETA makes a loss!

91

PRODUCT COSTING

CHALLENGE THE SYSTEM
SCRAP

Are scrap costs analysed by product?

- or treated as 'below-the-line'?
- or prorated?

Scrap should be analysed by product and by cause.

You need this information to focus your drive against scrap!

PRODUCT COSTING

CHALLENGE THE SYSTEM

ESTIMATES

When producing budgeted product costs, the direct material, direct labour and production overhead costs have to be estimated. The estimate is usually compiled by reference to past cost experience as recorded in the costing system.

Get it right!

Incorrect records will perpetuate problems.

Is there sufficient feedback of actual cost information to those who compiled the estimate for them to learn from their mistakes?

The most expensive mistake is the one nobody learns from!

PRODUCT COSTING

CHALLENGE THE SYSTEM
SPURIOUS ACCURACY!

Beware of decimals!

Don't be conned by delusions of accuracy!

Remember there is no such thing as **the** cost of a product!

... so why does your accountant insist on producing costs to 3 decimal places ...? It is far better to be approximately right than precisely wrong.

PRODUCT COSTING

STEP 3: BE FLEXIBLE

- Cost information must be adjusted according to
  the decision being taken

- Which costs are relevant to the decision?
  - Product cost (from the costing system)?
  - Incremental (or marginal) cost?
  - Replacement cost?
  - Opportunity cost?

- What will be the impact to the business
  - in the short-term?
  - in the long-term?

One costing system cannot provide a
quick-fix to all your decision-making needs.

PRODUCT COSTING

BE FLEXIBLE

EXAMPLE I: MAKE OR BUY?

- A key factor in the make or buy decision is the comparison between the purchase price and the in-house cost

- What **is** the in-house cost?

    - which costs would change?
    - costs that would not change are **irrelevant!**
    - what would be the impact on working capital?
    - what effect would there be on capacity/space/occupancy costs?
    - what opportunity costs are there? etc

Remember to look at the long-term as well as short-term implications.

Don't just use the product cost!

PRODUCT COSTING

BE FLEXIBLE
EXAMPLE II: MINIMUM ORDER QUANTITIES

- You require a widget to satisfy a customer order

- The supplier quotes £1 with a minimum order quantity of 50

- What is the cost of the widget?
  £1 or £50?

- If the other 49 will be used, then £1

  But beware

  If the other 49 have no predicted use, then the cost is £50

Which cost is appropriate when pricing the order?

Be prepared to adjust basic cost information.

PRODUCT COSTING

SUMMARY

- To manage a business you must

  Understand your products

- So you must understand the effect each product has on the business performance
- Critical decisions are taken based on product cost information

  Get it right!

APPENDICES

APPENDIX ONE

BUSINESS FINANCIAL MODEL

SOURCE OF FUNDS

- Businesses need long-term finance

- This comes from
  - Shareholders
  - Lenders
  - Reinvestment of profits

Accountant's term:
- Share capital
- Loan capital
- Retained profits

| SHARE CAPITAL | LOAN CAPITAL | RETAINED PROFITS |

SOURCE OF FUNDS

BUSINESS FINANCIAL MODEL

USE OF FUNDS

- The long-term finance is used to provide

		Accountant's term
Facilities/processes	-	Fixed assets
Products/services	-	Working capital

SHARE CAPITAL	LOAN CAPITAL	RETAINED PROFITS

SOURCE OF FUNDS

USE OF FUNDS

FACILITIES / PROCESSES	PRODUCTS / SERVICES
FIXED ASSETS	WORKING CAPITAL

APPENDIX ONE

BUSINESS FINANCIAL MODEL

MAKING PROFIT

- By using the fixed assets, the working capital investment generates products that can be sold

- Once **all** costs have been met and interest, tax and dividend allowed for, then any profit left over can be reinvested into the business

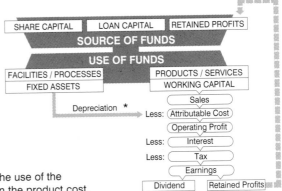

SHARE CAPITAL	LOAN CAPITAL	RETAINED PROFITS

SOURCE OF FUNDS

USE OF FUNDS

FACILITIES / PROCESSES	PRODUCTS / SERVICES
FIXED ASSETS	WORKING CAPITAL

Depreciation *

Sales
Less: Attributable Cost
Operating Profit
Less: Interest
Less: Tax
Earnings

Dividend	Retained Profits

* Depreciation is a charge for the use of the fixed assets and is included in the product cost.

Note: This model is developed step by step in *The Balance Sheet Pocketbook*

APPENDIX TWO

PRODUCT COSTING EXAMPLE
CHOICE OF COST CENTRES

On page 85 it was stated that product costs will be affected by:

- number and definition of cost centres
- method of absorption
- basis of apportioning costs

The following example demonstrates some of their effects. Refer back to page 81 for the initial information.

Suppose you use a separate cost centre for materials to charge out purchasing, receiving costs, etc.

Additional information:

Production overheads:	£
Material related overheads	75,000
Labour related overheads	525,000
Total	600,000
Planned material purchases	£750,000

The overhead absorption rates would now be:

Materials $\dfrac{£75,000}{£750,000} = 10\%$ Labour $\dfrac{£525,000}{15,000} = £35/\text{hour}$

PRODUCT COSTING EXAMPLE
CHOICE OF COST CENTRES

The revised product cost would be:

		£
Direct material		50
Direct labour		35
Production overhead:		
Material (£50 @ 10%)	5	
Labour (7 hours x £35/hour)	245	
		250
Product cost		335

Which is correct?

Has your business got it right?

APPENDIX TWO

PRODUCT COSTING EXAMPLE
CHOICE OF COST CENTRES

Example continued:

- Suppose you then separate machining from assembly?
- Additional information:

			£
Production overheads:	Material related overheads		75,000
	Labour related overheads:	Machining	400,000
		Assembly	125,000
	Total		600,000

Planned labour hours:	Machining	10,000 hours
	Assembly	5,000 hours

- The overhead absorption rates for labour would now be:

Machining $\dfrac{£400,000}{10,000}$ = £40/hour   Assembly $\dfrac{£125,000}{5,000}$ = £25/hour

- Product X requires   2 hours machining
                       5 hours assembly

PRODUCT COSTING EXAMPLE

CHOICE OF COST CENTRES

The revised product cost would be:

		£
Direct material		50
Direct labour		35
Production overhead:		
Material	5	
Machining (2 hours x £40/hour)	80	
Assembly (5 hours x £25/hour)	<u>125</u>	
		<u>210</u>
Product Cost		<u>295</u>

Another correct answer!

APPENDIX TWO

PRODUCT COSTING EXAMPLE
BASIS OF ABSORPTION

● The choice of absorption factor will also influence the product cost

Example:

Suppose in the previous example you decided to recover the machining overheads using machine hours rather than labour hours.

Additional information:

Planned machining hours   16,000
Machine hours required for Product X   3 hours

The overhead absorption rate for machining would be:

$$\frac{£400,000}{16,000 \text{ hours}} = £25/\text{hour}$$

PRODUCT COSTING EXAMPLE

BASIS OF ABSORPTION

The revised product cost would be:

		£
Direct material		50
Direct labour		35
Production overhead:		
Material	5	
Machining (3 hours x £25)	75	
Assembly	<u>125</u>	
		205
Product Cost		<u>290</u>

Spoilt for choice!   £365? £335? £295? £290?

Which would **you** use for **your** tender?

Don't forget there is no such thing as **the** product cost.

Look for the method that is appropriate to your business and the decision to be made.

About the Authors

Anne Hawkins, BA, ACMA is a Management Accountant with a first class honours degree in Business Studies. Anne has progressed from this strong knowledge base to gain senior management accounting experience within consumer and industrial product industries. As a Training Consultant she develops and presents finance programmes to Directors and Managers from all sections of industry.

Clive Turner, ACMA, MBCS is Managing Director of Structured Learning Programmes Ltd, established in 1981 to provide management consultancy and training services. Clive works with management to develop strategic business options. He participates in the evaluation process: designs the appropriate organisation structure and provides management development to support the implementation process. Clive continues to have extensive experience in delivering financial modules within Masters Programmes in the UK and overseas.

For details of support materials available to help trainers and managers run finance courses in-company, contact the authors at 3 Clews Road, Oakenshaw, Redditch, Worcs B98 7ST.

© Anne Hawkins and Clive Turner 1995
This edition published in 1995 by Management Pocketbooks Ltd. Reprinted 1997
14 East Street, Alresford, Hants. SO24 9EE
Printed in England by Alresford Press Ltd., Alresford, Hants. SO24 9QF   ISBN 1 870471 342

ORDER FORM

Your details

Name _____

Position _____

Company _____

Address _____

_____

_____

_____

Telephone _____

Facsimile _____

VAT No. (EC companies) _____

Your Order Ref _____

Please send me:

		No. copies
The Managing Budgets	Pocketbook	
The _____	Pocketbook	
The _____	Pocketbook	
The _____	Pocketbook	
The _____	Pocketbook	
The _____	Pocketbook	
The _____	Pocketbook	

MANAGEMENT POCKETBOOKS
14 EAST STREET ALRESFORD
HANTS SO24 9EE UK
Tel: +44 (0)1962 735573
Fax: +44 (0)1962 733637
E-mail: pocketbks@aol.com